THE DESTINED EXTINCTION OF ZIONISM

GREGORY HEARY

NO PAGE IN YOUR BOOK OF DEEDS ON THE DAY OF TERROR SHOULD BE BLANK OR WASTED WITH SINS EVEN IF IT IS ERASED BY ALLAH DUE TO REPENTANCE.

2

Our previous book "*The History of the Zionist State*" tracked the theological origins of the modern state of Israel dating back to over 500 years prior to its ruthless bloody creation and expounded upon some of its expansionist history. It is our hope that the toxicity of Zionism does not last another 500 years but we do not know the future and soothsaying is disbelief. This book is about the prerequisite conditions that will likely cause the destined end of Zionism which many hope and pray for, and how to achieve those conditions. Sadly some enemies of Zionism unintentionally aide Zionism due to how they attempt to combat it incorrectly. As a reminder, since Zionism did not take root in Palestine overnight then the solutions to this political weed in the holy land also may require time and concentrated effort. There are different timelines for how Zionism will end depending on many factors. Although to understand Zionism better we must examine their endgame goals and objectives if they win everything they strive for.

Zionism misuses fabled Jewish and Biblical prophecies of holy land being destined for Jewish ownership and government. There are no boundaries to this land and the projected maps always increase in size and the amount of land deemed holy which is up for grabs. Also because Jews wait for a future yet to come prophetic Messiah then any stipulated land boundaries according to Jews will change at any time when their "Messiah" says so, who could be anybody at any time according to their whims and desires. Thus even if negotiations were a theoretical possibility due to ignorant tolerance of this far-fecthed covenantal land grant then those boundaries, even if clearly demarcated and agreed upon, would not be permanent according to Jewish Zionism. Yet there is also another form of Zionism called Christian Zionism loudly championed by Israel's strongest military ally the USA and to a lesser extent other European countries.

The theory of Christian Zionism is linked to Christian Apocalypticism as taught by Christopher Columbus and others. The Christian doctrine is that Jesus will come back quickly to stop the hated Jews from ruling the holy land, and it is at that point in time Christians plan to betray their Jewish Zionist cause to fight the immoral Zionists, their false Messiah, and convert the Jews they formerly militarily allied with, to Christianity by force under the command of Jesus himself. So basically Christians have allied with the devil to try to force God's hand, as they see it, only to then side against their evil allies at the last minute. Such a treacherous plot of religious deception is immoral on the face of it betraying the prophetic religion of Jesus. Just as Zionism and it's genocidal blueprint betrays the prophetic religion of Abraham, Moses and David. Meanwhile the Muslims happened to be living in Palestine and most of the rest of this holy land and are caught between the apocalyptic Jews and the apocalyptic Christians both of whom have nothing but enmity for the Muslims. The enmity Jews and

Christians together have for Muslims is greater than their enmity for each other. Thus this creative insane double-betrayal Jew-Christian military alliance is made possible only due to their extreme hatred of Muslims.

Jews seek to benefit from the military alliance short-term to gain power for further future conquest. Christians seek to lose military assets and morality temporarily in order to trigger a rapid apocalyptic scenario. However the Doomsday theories of both groups are erroneous and false due to coming from distorted man-made scriptures and misinterpretations of those scriptures instead of the actual prophetic prophecies regarding the end of time. Yet rather than describe the proper end scenario of the world, if we entertain for the sake of argument either the Jewish or Christian apocalyptic fantasies neither scenario ends well for either group. For once the theoretically future Jewish Messiah comes the Jews will have to wage world war against all other countries simultaneously for Judaism. Thereby losing all the military allies they have so far. This is what they fear and publicly say will lead to their destruction yet it is the same exact scenario they hope for simultaneously. So theoretically they hope for their worst fears to come true, to be in a violent Zionist versus everyone world.

Meanwhile if we examine the Christian double-cross scenario it doesn't get better for them either. For if the Zionist cause is so wrong and evil that helping it will trigger God sending prophet

Jesus to earth to fight against it, then obviously the all-knowing God will not leave the Christian culprits off the enemy list as they naively think. For turning the other cheek as they say Jesus preached is not comparable to allying with genocidal Jews to force a prophetic showdown to happen as soon as possible. Basically the Christian Zionist theory is to be so bad that Jesus himself comes back to kick butt, but then once the Christians see Jesus angry at them then they expect to repent on the spot and be forgiven while they butcher the Jews they supported for hundreds of years prior. Such would be a similar case as if those who made the Golden Calf during the time of Moses where aided by people who didn't really worship the Golden calf sinfully but just helped build it to force prophet Moses to return faster with the law they intend to keep once Moses returned without being blameworthy. Such a mythical category never existed where doing bad is justified because of "good intentions".

I propose it is much better for the USA and Christian world if rather than join the Jews and Zionists (who they label disbelievers/killers of Christ) to fight the Muslims (who believe Jesus is a prophet) they should look to their ultimate future. They believe it will one time be morally best to oppose Zionism religiously and militarily. So the only real difference of opinion is the timing on when to end that devilish alliance before you burn in this life and the next. Theologically as Muslims believe in the prophethood of Jesus, true Christians prefer Muslim victory rather than

Zionist victory. While even a Christian Crusader victory is more preferable to humanitarians than Zionism as history proves. So why don't non-Muslims realize the destined fate of Zionism and plan for their self-interest even if stubborn upon disbelief in Islam?

The best case for Zionists of both Jewish and Christian varieties is Muslim extinction from Morocco to China but then what? Muslims and Christians agree Prophet Jesus will come back. But even if a bigoted Christian errantly thinks 100% of Muslims are such evil devils as to justify this Jewish alliance so Muslims go extinct if they continue crusading and funding Zionism, what happens next if they accomplish that goal? If Muslims do go extinct and Jews get all the holy land they desire and more as a "buffer zone", what happens? Will the Christian world then finally turn on the Jews who will then be ruling over a massive empire larger than any they have ever been recorded to have before historically? So at the height of Jewish might then Christians will finally decide that since it is a exclusively Jew and Christian world it is eventually time to quarrel and settle the issues once and for all? Do you think the Christians will have the advantage in such a scenario when they can't even turn against the Jews today? What would the Jews do?

There are 2 options for that fictional theoretical Jewish Empire. Either they expand their war to Christian territory, which they already do in Palestine, or the Jews commit to world peace with Christians/Buddhists/Hindus/Atheists

/ Animists all getting along without Muslims in the picture anymore. Realistically the Abrahamic Faiths movement teaches this scenario without Muslim extinction in theory, but in practice the Abrahamic Faiths fallacy is only tolerant of Jewish practices. For what do Jews, Christians and Muslims have in common? Only the Jewish prophets so anything not Jewish the Jews will say "This is not part of our shared religious stuff, so not allowed." Thus ultimately the Abrahamic Faiths movement is a way for the whole world to become Jewish in everything except name. For Judaism in practice is the only thing allowed under the Abrahamic Faiths umbrella of "tolerance", but they just don't call it what it really is. But then if we do all become Jews in practice under this

Abrahamic peace process plot how long will this peace last? When Jesus comes back will he agree to the Abrahamic theory? Will the Iron Dome, Nukes, Drones, Tanks, Guns all be deactivated and returned to their Christian countries of origin once the threat of Muslims is gone? Or will all those weapons Christians gave to Zionists be turned against Prophet Jesus the 2nd time around? Imagine if Prophet Jesus asks who gave the Jews such weaponry? What if he got hurt? Or will Jesus say he is at peace with the vast Jewish Empire and the slanderous disbelieving Jews governing Jerusalem, Bethlehem, Nazareth and all the holy land? Will Prophet Jesus beg for a Israeli tourist visa? Or will Jesus come back with a sword in genocidal fashion choosing rather to kill all Jews who refuse to believe in the prophethood of Jesus?

At least Adolf Hitler put Jews to work in camps allowing temporary albeit humiliating inhumane respite before death, but prophet Jesus is predicted to be much less gentler with Jews than that. Prophet Jesus both truly and falsely is prophesied by all pro-Jesus religions to come back with genocidal intent to make all of Judaism 100% extinct. So isn't it better for those equipping the Zionists to stop sooner rather than later? Why give the nation and army that fights prophet Jesus more ammunition in advance? Do you think God will bless nations giving weapons to those preparing to fight prophets? Has God blessed America and/or other allies of Israel since allying with it? Or have they declined in many areas ever since entering into alliances with Zionism?

Regarding the genocidal Zionist state of Israel today being a "sign of the end" this is not something Islam teaches. The Islamic "signs of the end" are clear and Muslims can not twist them try to make them seem as though they all foretell our current times. Many minor signs have come and some haven't, but at the time of this writing zero of the major signs have occurred. All the minor signs must come before the major signs, and then the major signs will rapidly take place. While such stuff is important to know, how you live is more important because for most of us our end is when we die and we will likely die before the end of the world, so we should live the same regardless of how much time the world has left. Seriously if someone proved to you 100% that the end of the world was guaranteed to happen in 45 days what would you do differently? Your lifestyle shouldn't really change at all. You should be doing good and avoiding evil all the time and this is why God hasn't revealed to us the exact time, because if we knew then we'd be lazy in life saying, "*Hey, relax, just enjoy your life and have lots of fun, stop acting like it's the end of the world.*" People who make such statements are the types who know they will be in big trouble when this worldly life does end. Whereas since our personal end is more likely to occur to us today than the end of the world, we should be acting on a daily basis like we are about to meet our maker by being repentant and pious, so we aren't in big trouble when it happens. Acting "like it's the end of the world" doesn't mean acting crazy, or uptight, it means being virtuous. As a sidenote, only the worst of disbelievers will be alive at the end of the world. This is because when the true religion is no longer available there will be no point for God letting the world continue since humans are created to worship him. Soon after God permanently removes guidance from the world it will be destroyed. So if you plan on going to paradise and not going to hell, then you will die before the end of the world. Prepare for your end today, because today might be your day. Those who support Israel today think it is a sign of the end and do so for religious reasons, just as the popes told Christians to crusade because it was allegedly a sign of the end, although most today pretend it's not for religious reasons because they want secular support. Most unislamic end times theories are specially crafted to lead one to think that certain people should be killed, or to promote political agendas, or that their religious books eerily and flawlessly predicted everything up until the present and thus must also predict the future, or that the end of the world will surely come in your lifetime so you must pay attention to them and join/ buy their stuff which has information you *"need to know"*. It doesn't benefit the soul to know such end time prophecies much if one is already negligent regarding their daily life. For the end of your life is more important to you than the end of the world, so prepare for the end of your life before the end of the world; just in case you die before earth.

As a disclaimer we must explain that being Anti-Zionist and Anti-Israel is not anti-semitic. Even being anti-Jew isn't being anti-semitic. Semites are the descendants of Shem who was the son of Prophet Noah. Most Semites are not Jewish, and ironically most Arabs are Semites. Anti-Semitic means you hate a person's race, Anti-Jewish means you hate their religion, Anti-Zionist means you hate their politics. This is why it's so important to know what words mean before we use them. Especially words like Radical Judaism, Radical Christianity or Radical Atheism. But I'm confident you are so familiar with those words they need not be defined. The Jewish Rabbis within Israel are against the existence of the state of Israel and as Jewish Anti-Zionists they get harmed by the Zionist state when they publicly protest it and prove through religious texts that the Jews lost their claim to statehood and that God has forbidden a Jewish state according to Jewish Scriptures. Furthermore one cannot be a Muslim or even a Christian without having Jewish heroes and role models. So the whole Anti-Semitic ploy of Zionists, many of whom are not even ethnically true Jews, to protect criticism of genocidal policy and Zionist discrimination is part of the plot and tactics used by devious devils to protect their ill-gotten reputation of immunity from shameful blame. The anti-Semitic trope is a joke often used in conjunction with the Abrahamic faiths disguise. Which again is purely racist if you consider that Abraham called to worshipping the Creator and obeying whichever future prophets that are sent and never limited the religion to Abraham only. Thus the Abrahamic Faiths movement is religious racism partial to Abraham, taking the God of Abraham out of the picture entirely because the God of Abraham is known to be intolerant of disbelievers and to have sent extra prophets after Abraham. Anyways just as not all Germans during Hitler's era should be killed because of Adolf Hitler or Nazism, not all Jews or Zionists should be killed due to Zionism. Not even all Nazis were killed due to Nazism. Yet Adolf Hitler made it a creed that anyone against Hitler or Nazism was by default an enemy trying to destroy Germany and all Germans. Even if they were German Nazis themselves. As some German Nazis even famously tried assassinating Hitler, but Hitler survived and labeled them genocidal anti-Germans just as Zionists label their opponents with the anti-Semitic and terrorist label. Hence Zionism, despite claiming to hate Nazism that fueled their rise to power, actually incorporates many tactics used by Nazi's in their own public relations campaigns to achieve Zionist goals.

The noises claiming opposition to Zionism come from many places yet despite their glamorous clamor no progress is found. But what does the picture of opposition look like today? It is similar to the disunity faced by Yusuf ibn Ayyubi aka Saladin who liberated the holy land from Crusader control. Back then Saladin did not start by battling Christians, that happened last after religious unity was achieved. Today we have Khawarij of all kinds widespread sinfully condemning rulers promoting revolutions intentionally and unintentionally through ignorance. Then there are several Shiite states spread throughout the land preaching Shirk and Kufr while fools feigning good intentions wish to unite anti-Zionists with such a greater evil against the lesser evil of Zionism. As I witnessed one such "nasheed artist" who started their career with a song praising the Sahabah including Abu Bakr and Umar but in one of their latest videos are hyping up a crowd waving Iranian Shiite flags rhythmically singing "Free Palestine!" thus changing creeds with the crowd contradicting their previous religious doctrines to *unite with devils to fight other devils*. Such "good people" motivated to do things should not do so! The munafiqeen harm us more when they battle alongside us. Insane idiots even moreso! If you are so strong you are helpful prove it by lifting the blanket before dawn daily to do tahajjud, dua and fajr where you are supposed to. Most can't do that or even sleep on their right side as the prophet taught us to do while sleeping. The biggest problem isn't the double standards of fake Zionist diplomacy and "ceasefires". It's that the masses of lunatics "speaking up for Palestine" keep triggering reactionary devilish chains of events never cease firing people up to new levels of sin and stupidity in the name of problem-solving. Ironically prayer beads were invented by Kharijites and Taqleedi

Madhhabism was invented by the Shia, thus showing how deep Bida has penetrated the Ummah. Then there are the Sufis quick to contaminate ears with innovative nasheeds of music and hypnotic hyper emotional "vocal only" songs all of which are bida, of which anti-zionism is a favorite subject they sing about while riling rageful demeanors spreading anger and sorrow for no good reason. Meanwhile the secularist Munafiqs, whether preaching Coexistence or other types of futile doomed non-religious resistance fail to comprehend pure prophetic religion being the solution. Then the protesting pro-voting democratically minded often pose a bigger threat to Islam and Muslims than the Zionist Jews do if they only knew the danger of the doctrines they embraced which contaminate all races. So when the big picture of Zionism is viewed, and I myself am incapable of seeing everything in that picture or describing it in this book, the innovations that are introduced to combat Zionism if left to survive will be worse for the Muslims and the rest of the world even if Zionism dies. For if Zionism vanishes but the innovations remain then we will have suffered greatly as a result of such spiritual plagues being unleashed to combat an external temporary enemy.

On the other hand if Zionism isn't defeated then perhaps in 2300 CE there will be a Zionist Thanksgiving tradition in Abrahamic manner similar to the fictional Thanksgiving tradition in America, where a mythological party of Christian Pilgrims and Native

Americans is celebrated by the conquerors of America. Native Americans suffer in disgraceful shame and colonization unable to even voice historical accurate facts that dispel the "Thanksgiving" Interfaith party that never took place. Thanksgiving is a myth invented by colonists hundreds of years after colonization as history books often get written by the military who conquers, or at least the popular history books do. Historically President Abraham Lincoln invented Thanksgiving on October 3rd, 1863 pretending characters like Squanto and other 'indians' ate a meal with colonizers hundreds of years earlier to soothe national sentiment over the American Civil War ending and unification being militarily enforced, as well as to quell Native American unrest due to the genocidal Dakota War of 1862. The reality is America was ruthlessly colonized through immoral sinful manipulative treacherous treaties and genocidal wars, there was never any Pilgrim-Indian Thanksgiving dinner in all of history. The American Thanksgiving is less likely than a Zionist-Palestine Thanksgiving approving Jewish illegal settlements of the 1900s and earlier and later, yet still hundreds of millions of Americans hundreds of years later celebrate such a fictional narrative with joy on annual basis. So perhaps in a few centuries people may say how Zionists and Palestinians worshipped together in harmony in Jerusalem ever since Israel was founded, ignoring all the conflict we constantly experience in our era. For those thinking such a theory is far-fetched just remember the hundreds of millions of Native Americans nearly entirely extinct themselves and mockingly characterized as a cultural symbol of uncivility as a result.

True Muslims know that protesting and voting is not the solution to Zionism. Therefore unashamedly I and others fully agree with kafir policies of deporting and imprisoning "pro-Palestine protesters" etc, despite vehemently opposing Zionism more than they do. This is because it is unlawful in Islam to protest even if in a non-Muslim country because it's not a correct method of waging war or improving the government, rather it is imitation of kuffar and involves many sins as well. It is perfectly legal even if hypocritical for non-Muslim

disbelievers to prohibit anti-zionist
activity if they choose to. So why
stubbornly expose their hypocrisy for
other than Allah's Islamic religion? For
example the protesters get injured,
arrested, a criminal record, debanked,
and severely oppressed as a result of
protest activity. Rather than argue if it's
fair, it's known to be a risk not worth
the reward. Why would someone want
to lose all the goodness they have in life
to sinfully protest in ways that can
destroy their health, job prospects, hijra
opportunity and basic abilities to live.
For what? Do they risk this to do a
fard/wajib act of worship? Or to avoid
doing kufr or shirk? No, they do this for
something not even obligatory or
recommended but actually sinful and
wasteful when examined. If 1% of the
millions marching in streets would

lawfully emigrate, go to a Muslim country enlist in the military, and privately (not publicly) inform their commanders they are preparing for war with Zionists this may yield results. That is a much better way to make progress than protests even if protests were halal of which they are all haram from multiple angles, even if just for the fact of not praying salat in the masjids. Today Muslim leaders where Islam is the national religion don't have 95% of the male population showing up to pray Fajr in the masjids when athan is called as compared to Jumuah. Now what if hypothetically Muslim communities agreed for a surprise unity attack on Zionism to start next Shawwal 2nd, BUT only if 1% of Muslims made accepted duas to Allah for victory while fulfilling all the conditions of Tawheed, Taqwa,

Bir, Ikhlas etc. What if the Muslim leaders required all obligatory salat to be prayed by men in the masjid and women at home, all who are able to fast Ramadan, with no gossip, no music, no vulgarity, no sports, no TV, no Zina, no dating, no flirting, no masturbating, no gambling, no lying even if joking. All major and minor sins listed and those unlisted had to be abstained from for just a few months prior to Shawwal for the invasion of the Zionist state upon total Muslim community unity. This invasion would be launched until victory was attained or martyrdom or the Ummah stopped their improved Islam and returned to sin. Would you be the person to comply with these conditions for the sake of defeating Zionism? For how long? What if Allah made that the solution? Would you choose another? What if Allah set a higher # than just 1% doing that and said 5% of Muslims must act right? What if it was 10%, or 25%, or 50% or 75%? What if Allah is commanding an angelic army preparing to aide us once we hit that target number of obedience for as long as it is maintained? In that situation is protesting or voting or boycotting going to fix it? What about commenting on the internet? No? Factually Allah did not make a plan where once X# of people do forbidden sinful nationalist protests then he will unite the Ummah and unleash angelic fury if just 1 more idiot chants 1 more stupid slogan. Rather protests set the cause of Islam backward. Idiots conflate Islam with Palestine due to such protesting when Islam is free from nationalism. Since it is well within the right and law for any nation to ban, deport or imprison political destabilizers even if hypocritical and contradictory to the false faith of freedom on their law books, it is unfair to expect other than punishment be meted out to protesters. Even if Zionists didn't punish protesters Allah would do so through other means. But sadly because of these pro-Palestine protests being conflated with Islam and Muslims by association, then being Muslim practicing Islam becomes more likely to be banned and punished in such environments as an ignorant political precaution. Then what? Wouldn't you rather have been able to preach the salvation of Islam in USA and elsewhere but be silent on Palestine while people worship Allah, make Hijrah and increase the # of Muslims in the world?

Or is it better for America to ignorantly ban Islam and Muslim America goes extinct and the masjids all close and get destroyed with wealth confiscated, people deported and killed or worse converted to Kufr because of anti-Zionist activity being strictly outlawed and conflated with Islam? Which is truly better preaching Islam or preaching anti-Zionism?

Kufr/Disbelief is a worse crime than the genocide of Muslims. So for all those protesting Muslims, they should be more outraged at a prayer to other than Allah than they are at Muslims dying. Hajjaj bin Yusuf killed more Muslims than Netanyahu, including killing Sahabah inside of Mecca and destroying the Kaba. Yet the peaceful anti-Zionist pro-Palestine million dollar donator to

charity is much worse and more hated
by Allah for a single missed Salat or
prayer to Jesus or any other type of Kufr
and Shirk committed than Hajjaj is.
Thus true Muslims gladly support
stopping pro-Palestine protesting in the
lands of non-Muslims and even moreso
in Muslim lands. Only extremism and
evil comes from such protests and
misprioritization. Both the elements of
innovative Ikhwani unity and Khariji
Khurooj are present in protesting and
the other ills spread by such crimes are
too innumerable to count. Particularly
in Muslim lands it is even worse to
protest because it is even more sinful to
oppose the rulers publicly insincerely.
Such sinful rebellion doesn't merely
occur via guns but with tongues as well
both offline and online. Rather than
backbite, gossip, condemn and critique

Muslim rulers weakening them thereby proper Muslims make supplication for the benefit of Muslim rulers globally hoping for their peaceful rectification. The cursing of Muslim rulers must be replaced by blessings being invoked for them prior to unity becoming reality. On the contrary Khurooj being waged against them instills cowardice among both ruler and ruled alike and such khurooj(rebellion) by typing or tongue is all accursed sinful slander or backbiting even if what is said is true.

Fundamentally the priority is Tawheed as the prophet taught, not the end of oppressive bloodshed or land grabbing. The prophets never came with a goal of world peace. Prophets came with the message of paradise for Muslims and Hellfire for non-Muslims. The command of Allah to call to this prophetic message is obligatory. Prophets did not command Muslims to chant for liberating Palestine or any land anywhere. The Sahahbah conquered such lands incidentally as a minor blessing due to obedience to the major objectives of elevating the religion of Allah upon earth. The most important matters consist of the Shahada, the Salat, the Zakat, the Saum, the Hajj, Character, banning music, banning drugs, banning superstitions like Luck, banning gambling, banning tribalism and nationalism and combatting all evil. Yet today Muslims do the opposite of what Islam teaches to free a land we didn't earn, and never deserved for Allah to grant us. For the whole world is worth less than a mosquito's wing to Allah. So whether it is land or lives, it is not worth what religion is worth. But people want to do everything else in the world to combat Zionism except get religious in their life.

For example an influential community member I personally used to be acquainted with held a pro-Palestine event recently to protest a local bank branch having invited a Zionist representative to a fundraising dinner. I felt this was disastrous hypocrisy because this same person previously worked for this bank himself for years building software for them despite their usurious practices. Allah is at war with usurers as is well known from the Quran but Allah being at war with the bank was not enough to deter his employment, but after he got another job he felt them having 1 IDF guest attend a public dinner at 1 local branch was worth them mobilizing the Muslim community to cause a scene writing letters "for Palestine" rather than for Allah. The plan was to get as many Muslims as possible to send a letter to condemn their dinner event due to this pro-Zionist guest. Now honestly is a single bank in America cancelling a dinner due to Muslims being offended by one of their guests attending going to do anything at all to solve Zionism? If so why not also condemn the usury too? Or better yet do as Allah commands us to do and request the bank staff change their religion? No, we allegedly are not powerful or influential enough for such important tasks as those. But even if the bank had reacted better than crazily hoped for then what? Does Palestine have a celebration because 1 local bank cancelled a dinner party or uninvited a guest? More likely the bank would get pissed off and be less receptive and less respectful to Muslims and Islam making future dawah even harder to do. So truly no good is done from "*doing anything, as little as it is, to help the cause*". In actuality the cause of Allah against Zionism and Disbelief and Oppression is actually harmed by such ignorant actions as is easily anticipated. At best nothing would change and time/efforts would be wasted. Yet if such destructive plots actually worked and the event were theoretically cancelled as rudely demanded then what? Then the idiots grow in confidence and delusion and numbers increasing influence and can do even more damage claiming to be fixing problems not seeing how they are making problems bigger.

Even I may be guilty of unqualified reckless input adding to the chaotic cultural clash making the matter worse. Because the truly evil outcome for Islam is not loss of Muslim numbers, land, wealth, public image reputation, or time. But the true loss is in the sins that will haunt both Muslims and Kuffar on the Day of Judgement. Speaking of Allah without knowledge is standard practice due to the hot button issue of Palestine or Zionism. Yet speaking about Allah without knowledge is one of the greatest sins of all time. So once again even if Zionism went extinct overnight, what about all the heretical innovations, sins and unislamic standards that became popular due to the movements against Zionism. The "cures" are worse than the disease. Such cures that are harmful to us today include Nationalism, Allying with Kuffar, Music, Terrorism, Rebellion, Voting, Picture-making, Anger for beings lesser than Allah and many more. Just consider which is worse for a moment, hurting Palestinians in the Holy Lands and their cause or harming the Messenger of Allah and his cause? Of which the Messenger of Allah famously told Umar bin Khattab how nobody truly believes until the Messenger of Allah is more beloved to them than everything after Allah, including themselves. But don't stop there for we cannot forget Allah. Which is worse to do, war against the Palestinians or war against Allah? Do you understand yet what I say? Is it not much worse than what a Zionist does when an isolated peaceful Christian

monk stands to pray in their monastery?
Yes!

Quran 19:90-92

تَكَادُ ٱلسَّمَٰوَٰتُ يَتَفَطَّرْنَ مِنْهُ وَتَنشَقُّ ٱلْأَرْضُ وَتَخِرُّ ٱلْجِبَالُ هَدًّا (٩٠) أَن دَعَوْاْ لِلرَّحْمَٰنِ وَلَدًا (٩١) وَمَا يَنۢبَغِى لِلرَّحْمَٰنِ أَن يَتَّخِذَ وَلَدًا (٩٢)

The heavens almost rupture therefrom and the earth splits open and the mountains collapse in devastation (90) That they attribute to the Most Merciful a son. (91) And it is not appropriate for the Most Merciful that He should take a son. (92)

But do these "Muslim" pro-Palestine activists act like such monks praying are much worse than bloodthirsty Zionists? Even if they agree verbally they are worse, their attitudes don't match their stated beliefs. What do they say is the solution to such a bigger problem than Zionism? Do they say we must fight them too? No, that's illegal and against the laws of Jihad. But what about protests outside the monastery or writing hundreds of complaint letters to the monks? Or boycott them blocking streets, shouting slogans? Or what about cursing them? Do pro-Palestine activists suggest doing any of that to deal with one petty weak unknown unpopular uninfluential financially poor unhealthy old guy? If they can't do nothing for the sake of Allah against such a singular major criminal monk in total isolated weakness when Allah is concerned about it and Allah commands peaceful dawah then why do the pro-Palestine or Anti-Zionists do so much against Zionism to fight against one of the biggest devilish international military alliances ever known? They can't do nothing to stop the evil weak devils next door that they know about but they are willing to do any and everything they can to take on the "biggest mischief makers" in the world today? They cannot curse the monk in a monastery but they can dare curse an innocent automobile driver they blocked the roadway for during their sinful protests? Do these devils not realize they are devils due to how they are fighting devils? In reality most of the anti-Zionist groups are more mischievous than the Zionists because such Muslim pro-Palestinian causes hijack Islam moreso than the Khariji terrorists and Shiite terrorists combined. Whereas Moses with his back against the sea facing Pharaoh's wrathful army never returned to the Khariji method. Even with 100% unity on the impending battlefield with no known alternative but fight or flee, surrender to Pharaoh and his desires or surrender to Allah. Moses obeyed his Lord every step of the way to Paradise repentant with remorse.

 Shia are well known as enemies to Muslims and are worse than Jews. So Sunni Muslim leaders are wary to act in ways that expose the Muslims to Shiite plots even in the case of Palestine. Simply put Muslim armies know if they attack and miraculously beat Zionism then the Shiite states will attack the Muslims at the most opportune strategic moment. Or worse the Shiites would ally with the Sunnis against the Jews and if Zionism were defeated by a Sunni-Shiite alliance the resulting religious amalgamation would be much worse than if Sunnis were ruled by Zionists. For being friends with devils is more dangerous than being an enemy that is oppressed or subjugated to devils. Its better to be beaten by devils every day of the week than be friends with them once. Such catastrophic pollution of religion by blending Shiism and Islam would destroy the pure prophetic religious creed and practices with Bida. Yet even such a risky recipe could be easily repairable over time by a return to the Quran and Sunnah as understood by the Salaf us-Salih. But the Pro-Palestine hijackers are blending Islam/Muslims spreading Bida, Kufr, Shirk and Sins and claiming it is Islamic, Sunni and even Salafi sometimes. Such false labels given to unprophetic tactics are most dangerous and the hardest to fix over the longest timeframe before we can ever return to the prophetic creed and deeds. For even if we return to our deen after befriending devils like the Shia and the West and the whole unislamic world against Zionism to fix Palestine, isn't it easier to just skip the corruption and multi-faith unholy alliances and never have to undergo a painful stressful long reformation effort? Instead of poisoning ourselves for thousands of years to kill Zionism "quickly" is not patiently enduring the Zionist onslaught defending against it as best as Islam allows expecting reward from Allah better than bringing ruin to the Ummah for the sake of theoretically fighting Zionism in a novel fast-paced manner?

Islam doesn't say Muslims can't do anything at all against Zionism. Muslims must just prioritize correctly with priorities taught by Allah and the prophets. Plus your personal location, age, gender, strength, wealth, role in the world also greatly determine your ability to do anything about anything. If you, like me, are an average peasant in the world power rankings then you must be realistic and accept the role Allah gave you in what your actual daily responsibilities are.

Allah will ask everyone on the Day of Judgement about many things they are 100% responsible to control and improve in their life. For most people Zionism is not something they will be asked about first, if at all. It probably won't even be asked about in the top 100 questions or the first 100 hours of questioning.

Abu Huraira reported:

The Messenger of Allah said,

"The first action for which a servant of Allah will be held accountable on the Day of Resurrection will be his prayers. If they are in order, he will have prospered and succeeded. If they are lacking, he will have failed and lost. If there is something defective in his obligatory prayers, then the Almighty Lord will say:

See if My servant has any voluntary prayers that can complete what is insufficient in his obligatory prayers. The rest of his deeds will be judged the same way."

Sunan al-Tirmidhi 413 Grade: Sahih

Who amongst us isn't already in trouble based on the first question? Are you not afraid of answering that? But you feel Zionism is such an important topic? By feeling so emotional about the Zionist plot you have already fallen into the trap of Shaitan without realizing it.

Even before that first question about Salat comes there are 3 questions in the graveyard. So for you or me to worry about Zionism which may be the billionth topic on our list when we may not be able to answer the first question or the first three questions I'm asked about is literally insane ignorant irresponsibility. Maybe after you save yourself and your family from the hellfire then you can possibly think about thinking about superhero activities, but as a super-sinner you must know your role.

If you cannot control your angry emotional reaction to Zionist news causing you to sin, in any way, then it is obligatory upon you to avoid what leads you to sin. So if you are incapable of Islamically reacting to news it becomes forbidden to learn the news and be updated until you learn the Quran and Sunnah and Islamically develop yourself. Even then since when are men allowed to look at imagery of women? When did pictures become allowed? People say gory images motivate awareness and donations. Yet this sensationalism is sinful regarding both dress codes and picture making. in Islam it's sinful to display videos or pictures of wounded or dead creatures, because it's a violation of their honor and involves image making. Islam teaches that nobody should make or see any videos or images of such stuff, yet Satan wants people to sin and thus gets humans to use imagery, usually in order to inspire more sins, but even if it were to motivate one to give charity Islam teaches it shouldn't be done. This is the beauty and wisdom of "strict" Islamic law in that it completely eliminates grotesque sensationalism, and gives dead creatures dignity. Images of victims desensitizes people making violent crime socially acceptable and it humiliates the creatures as well. It doesn't matter if you are using pictures of victims for good causes! It's sinful! I don't care if you are taking pictures of starving people so others give in charity or you're taking pictures of the dead or wounded to motivate people to fight oppressors. The prophets did not do this and they forbid it. No prophet was going around with imagery to motivate people to do the right thing or motivate them to do good or sympathize. Good people do good stuff without seeing pictures or videos. It is a violation of human rights to take pictures or videos of them when they are in a pitiful embarrassing condition. Nobody can say they are "doing it to help", you help people the way God said to and the way the prophets taught not by disobeying God and the prophets to "really show what's going on". Nobody needs to show, all they need to do is tell and the good people will do the right thing once the situation is known and the information is verified as true and reliable. The pictures and videos lead people to act because of their emotional reactions and stimuli of the senses turning people into beasts while we are supposed to be slaves of God who do what he wants for his sake. Believers aren't moved to action by imagery they are moved to action by their Creator. It doesn't matter how many pictures one sees the believer will not do anything unless it is what God wants, and it doesn't matter how little incentive the believer is given to do something if it's what God wants they will do it to the fullest without any external motivation. So those people taking pictures and videos of tragedy "for good causes" are just making matters worse and doing forbidden things that please Satan. Believers do the right thing in everything regardless, and that includes asking other to do the right thing in the right way which God and his prophets say is right. Many war-time photographers are war criminals in the sight of God, not that they should be harmed but many are doing sinful crimes during wars which God hates. Although this is something that should be common sense to people with good moral values. When did it become okay to publicly display human tragedy via pictures and videos? It was started by evildoers to motivate others to do evil things. If you really wanted to stop the constant bloodshed you'd want the pictures of victims to stop so society becomes less reactionary and impulsive upon being bombarded by Satan with emotional criminal imagery. Such sins always get started for "good causes" and then they do unimaginable damage in this life and in the afterlife. Do something good for humans by not taking pictures or videos of their tragedies and hardships. The more traumatic it is the more sinful such images/videos are. Traditionally Women under Islamic law are not even allowed to see their dead martyred relatives in most cases, yet today they see gory men's awra exposed for no permissible or beneficial reason. And likewise men see gory women's awra exposed for no permissible or beneficial reason. The Sunnah solution has become strange and true Salafis are strangers. As long as Muslims are using photos/music/nasheeds/sins to facilitate matters they will complicate the chaos making path to victory longer.

But people say things are different, now we are dealing with genocidal tyrants. Genocide or not doesn't change much at all. For even if Zionists followed all the military rules of Jihad perfectly fighting fairly etc, just raising the banner of Judaism in contrast to Islam and the belief in prophets Jesus and Muhammad, wouldn't they still deserve to be combatted? Many in the anti-Zionist movement would say no that just fighting Zionists due to religion alone would be wrong. Whereas true Muslims say yes they should be combatted even if they don't mix Zionism with genocide, racism, lying, cheating, etc. Such additions or subtractions doesn't change the warplan equation for true Muslims. So why do those extra things matter to so many across the world today? These "extras" only motivate insincere ignorants to get involved and hinder actual problem solving. It's not that Zionists are unaware that genocide is immoral and don't care, it's that they know doing genocide instead of fighting fair gets a whole bunch of idiots to fight against them on the other side who will sabotage their opponents unintentionally. Just as Osama bin Laden had done in sabotaging Islam

due to global oppression against
Muslims. So Zionists fighting sinfully in
a real sense helps the Zionists corrupt
the anti-Zionist movement due to the
backlash from fools joining the cause.

It is valuable to remember the clash
between Moses and Pharaoh. What was
Pharaoh? He was a genocidal tyrant
butcher much worse than any Zionist
regime. Pharaoh had Muslims enslaved
and killed and would have Muslims kill
their newborns with their own hands.
One such newborn that miraculously
escaped such a fate was Moses, who
later became a Messenger of Allah.
Prior to that Moses lived in Egypt ruled
by Pharaoh and there was a Muslim
resistance movement against Pharaoh's
injustice at that time too. Moses saw
such a resistance fighter getting into

trouble, similar to how protesters do today, so Moses reacted and helped his co-religionist who begged for help accidentally killing the Egyptian opponent. This is exactly what the Khawarij pitch as their gameplan today. But Moses called this a plot of Shaitan and sought sincere repentance. Then again a repeat scenario occurred, yet destiny saved Moses from further transgression and he fled as a homeless fugitive seeking asylum elsewhere without many prospects, begging Allah for good. Allah gave him so much good gradually over time that Moses ended up ruling a nation and defeating Pharaoh totally. How did that better than dreamed of political change happen? Via sincere lifelong repentance. After prophethood began Moses returned to Egypt, reluctantly in fear. Not fear for how to organize an armed rebellion or how to get enough votes to change the political situation. Moses feared he would fail spreading and practicing Islam as ordered by Allah. Pharaoh committed his greatest oppression by claiming divinity and disbelieving in the prophethood of Moses and Aaron. So private discussion continued. Eventually public showdowns occurred between the conglomerate of magicians and Moses. The magicians repented, believed and were killed on the spot, thus reducing the numbers of Muslims again. And guess what? The oppression got worse and worse for many years before victory ever occurred. But how did the hardship even begin?

Prophet Joseph's brothers plotted against him which led to his enslavement in Egypt and unjust imprisonment. Ultimately leadership was given by Allah to Prophet Joseph which led his family to move to Egypt. In Egypt, Joseph and his family were in the popular ruling class of society. Yet over time somehow the followers of Joseph's faith were oppressed to the point where Moses was making dua with his brother Aaron in dire conditions of needing divine aid. So what happened with Moses that resulted in victory? Can that same solution work against Zionism today?

If you listen to most anti-Zionist crowds today they'd have you think the best plan for Moses and his people would be to go to the state governed by Haman

(Pharaoh's loyal ally or lackey) and start voting against Haman or protesting that Haman stop supporting Pharaoh and boycott Haman until he complies changing his political allegiances. They'd recommend applying all kinds of pressure until Haman complies and becomes their ally against Pharaoh. But not so that Haman becomes a Muslim worshipping Allah. No, that's already deemed too hard and unrealistic to be achieved. Haman is just expected to side with Moses and support him despite disbelieving in Islam just due to the humanitarian reasons and economic/political pressure. And then what? What if Pharaoh crushed Haman and replaced him with an even eviler ally? What if Haman became more evil due to the Muslim protesters, votes, boycotts, songs, etc? Instead the solution for Moses that led to victory was truthful peaceful patient dawah until conditions determined and facilitated mass emigration. And it wasn't a scenario of let's flee and grow stronger, then come back and conquer militarily. It was true obedience to Allah. Then Allah solved the problems.

Then despite all the miracles and struggles during the path to victory, when Moses goes up a mountain to get additional religious rules to benefit/restrict human freedoms, the Jewish Muslims end up worshipping a golden cow in less than 40 days despite prophet Aaron being among them forbidding them from it. And then Moses returns and kills the very same people that he struggled so hard to liberate from Pharaoh's oppressive tyranny. The very same people who were victims of genocide for years, likely centuries, whom Allah sent 2 prophets to and miraculously liberated from slavery were ultimately butchered en masse in gory genocidal fashion. Moses killed a larger % of Jews than Pharaoh likely would have if he didn't drown. So the Muslim Jews escaped the butchery of Pharaoh only to be led to a greater butchery as Allah decreed. The majority of those whom all the Muslims prayed Allah would rescue and keep safe, who Allah then made victors over the evil superpower of the world, were subsequently slaughtered by the minority Muslim population which strictly obeyed Allah's religion sincerely. Why? Due to carrying the "extra baggage" the Muslims took from life in Egypt of which they imitatively turned their gold into an idol. Moses burned this idol and spread it into the sea which had consumed their enemies' corpses, thereby impoverishing the new nation destroying economic wealth built up for generations. Allah sent manna and quail to them for sustenance because they literally didn't have food or wealth to buy food with from others. Then what happened to those same heroes who defeated Pharaoh and killed their own apostates by hand? Once united with purity in their ranks did they conquer the world? Allah didn't destine that, as might be expected. Instead when commanded to conquer other kuffar the majority of the few who passed all prior tests refused to fight. So is this the miraculous victory the Muslims dream and pray for in the Holy land against the Zionist regime? Do they want a victory against oppression and disbelief the way Moses was granted victory? Or do they want one the way Muhammad was granted victory in Mecca? Of which when prophet Muhammad died years after the Meccan conquest the majority of Arabia apostated and had to be fought. So much bloodshed occurred during such apostate wars it was feared the Quran itself would be lost; due to the large numbers who were killed fighting former co-religionists who themselves had fought alongside them days before when fighting Quraish and the Jews. Are these prophetic victories the hopes of the Anti-Zionist movements today?

If the Anti-Zionist movement is not willing to fight and kill themselves the day after liberation from the Zionists if

Allah's religion ordains it then such a movement is not fit for Allah to give it victory in the first place against Zionists. How then would the case be with Moses if his people started worshipping the golden calf before Pharaoh was even defeated? Today many alleged Muslims are doing kufr/shirk/bida and sins with major legal consequences. And just like in Moses' time we have "resistance" movements like the proto-Khariji that Moses sinfully sympathized with to the extent of committing crime forbidden by Allah and the Pharaonic state alike. If the anti-Zionist fighter is not ready to later fight the liberated Palestinians for Allah's sake then any fight to free such Palestinians is no true Jihad, but nationalistic or something else which is sinful and other than for raising the word of Allah. Hence the Palestinian flag should be burned along with the Zionist flag if the Muslims burning flags were really sincere about elevating Islam instead of idiotic emotional nationalism. For Islam and Muslims are a global phenomenon and cause, so the P-word shouldn't carry much meaning in the life of a Muslim aside from being a standard geographic adjective. Especially when even the words Muhajir and Ansar were denounced by the Prophet when they caused unislamic beliefs and actions due to applying such labels. And not everyone labeled a "martyr" for the Islamic cause is a true martyr as Allah defines it even if it could be claimed as hopeful based on certain hadith or ayat.

We have a case in point that summarizes the present problems well.

Do you remember the former friend of mine announcing Muslims should voice displeasure with the local bank branch? In 2014 he was quoted in a collegiate news article as saying, "*You can't turn a blind eye to anyone, A brother in religion is closer than a blood brother.*" Yet 3 years later into our friendship in 2017 I discovered the local imam the mosque we both went to was a heretic who didn't believe Jews and Christians were kuffar/disbelievers. So I confronted the heretic about this error with this 3rd party "religious friend". Long story short I disagreed with this heresy, and after 3 months of trying and failing to correct the heretical error I asked this friend for help as he was much more influential in the community than me. I never got a reply to this day. I ended up getting banned from the mosque with a cease and desist order to never contact those mosque members or be seen there again. But as it pertains to this topic of Zionism, prior to my ban for "spreading disunity" this former friend offered to help me with my Tajweed Quran recitation in the midst of my battle with heresy. Of which disunity with people of different creeds and methodologies is treated like heresy with most anti-Zionist movements. Why help me with Tajweed when I insisted we unite on Tawheed and creed? Not that the topic of Tajweed is unimportant or irrelevant, but as my friend said, he wanted to teach me how little I know about Islam and how much I have to learn. I was grateful at least to be able to islamically improve in any way, though the help offered didn't seem to match my problems or priorities perfectly and felt insulting. Minimally it would humble me and prevent arrogance to be taught beneficial knowledge of any Islamic science. So we were about to begin to read the Quran and I asked what to read for my Tajweed test. He said to read surah fatihah the first chapter. I smiled and remembered the hadith from the sunnah to use a miswak or siwak toothbrush before reading the Quran.

Ali narrated Allah's Messenger said:

"When a servant of Allah uses the siwak, then stands to pray, an angel stands behind him. He listens to his recitation and draws close to him, until he places his mouth over his, such that nothing of the Quran leaves his mouth except that it enters the angel — so purify your mouths for the [recitation of the] Quran."

Source: Musnad Al-Bazzar 603
Grade: Sahih by Albani

Likewise Imām al-Ājurrī stated:

"I love that the one who wishes to recite the Quran in the night or day, that he should purify himself (wudoo) and use the miswāk, and that is in veneration of the Quran because he is reciting the speech of the Lord, the Mighty and Majestic. And because the angels draw close to him (or her) when he recites the Quran so an angel draws near to him, and if he had used the miswāk, he places his mouth over his, and each time he recites an āyah, the angel takes it into his mouth. And if he did not use the miswāk, the angel becomes distant from him. And it is not for you, O people of the Quran, to cause the angel to distance himself from you!"

(Alhlāq Hamlatul Qurān page 145)

So as I try to use siwak before my test, in the mosque itself I was shockingly told, *"Forget the Sunnah. Just read the Quran!"*

Now contemplate the gravity of this statement. Is it possible to even have a Quran without the Sunnah? Can you ever believe in the Quran without the Sunnah? How can it be that a Muslim in a mosque offering to "help" their Muslim friend with Tajweed recitation of Allah's uncreated speech can even think to say this let alone actually utter such a statement as to "forget the sunnah" while reading the Quran. Did any Sahaba or any of the Salaf say this? Rather they couldn't contemplate such evil as even being theoretical. Thus we live in a miserable era of hypothetically inconceivable ignorance and evil today. Hence the accursed methodology of: *"Forget about Allah and Tawheed and Islam, just free Palestine!"*

Thus many forget about the enemies of Allah and unite with Allah's enemies to allegedly fight other enemies of Allah. Although often throughout history Allah utilized some enemies of his to defeat other enemies who fight another enemy of Allah. Some enemies of Allah even gain victory over another enemy of Allah as Allah decrees, then both the victor and defeated die and go to eternal hell because they forgot Allah and the worship due to Allah. Hence the path of the believers has never been to join the enemies of Allah. Let our enemies fight each other without us getting involved with either. Also focusing on the enemies of Allah like Zionists is different than remembering Allah. True Muslims would rather lose to Zionists and maintain their Islamic faith than lose any tiny bit of their Islam in exchange for victory. Anti-Zionism has become obsessively extreme to heretical

extents for many Muslims in the world.
It is almost a rival religion to Islam itself
but worse because it is potentially
replacing Islam and changing the
definition of Islam/Muslim. While
Anti-Zionism has its place in a Muslim's
life, that place is of minor ranking when
all things are weighed correctly.

Quran 5:8

يَـٰٓأَيُّهَا ٱلَّذِينَ ءَامَنُواْ كُونُواْ قَوَّٰمِينَ لِلَّهِ شُهَدَآءَ بِٱلْقِسْطِ ۖ وَلَا يَجْرِمَنَّكُمْ شَنَـَٔانُ قَوْمٍ عَلَىٰٓ أَلَّا تَعْدِلُواْ ۚ ٱعْدِلُواْ هُوَ أَقْرَبُ لِلتَّقْوَىٰ ۖ وَٱتَّقُواْ ٱللَّهَ ۚ إِنَّ ٱللَّهَ خَبِيرٌۢ بِمَا تَعْمَلُونَ

*O you who have believed, be persistently
standing firm for Allāh, witnesses in justice,
and do not let the hatred of a people prevent
you from being just. Be just; that is nearer
to righteousness. And fear Allāh; indeed,
Allāh is [fully] Aware of what you do.*

Oftentimes in attempts to defeat or
combat Zionism many are unjust to
others, even themselves, and more

importantly they are unjust to the prophet Muhammad, his Sunnah and most importantly they are unjust to Allah our Judge. For what? To combat some crazy criminal Jews that have been doing some limited oppression, less than other groups have done, for a few decades, less time than other greater tyrants have oppressed better people?

The Zionists factually are better than Pharaoh and we are worse than Moses, who was patiently firm yet wise in sincerely attempting to guide Pharaoh to a just resolution to their conflict due to his conflict with Allah. Hence if Zionism is a punishment of Allah then we must repent so Allah eases our situation. And if Zionism is not a punishment of Allah but just a difficult test to determine the good from the bad and facilitate prophesied destiny, then the believer is patient in correctly changing themselves for the better regardless while striving in responsible Islamic means according to their ability.

A fundamental principle in Islam is that if individually you are unable to do a certain act of worship like Hajj, or Fasting or are unqualified as can happen with the duty of Zakat then such a person is excused and not punished for not attempting to solve problems they cannot solve at their level. They are not blameworthy in such circumstances. However they will be punished if emotionally they fanatically obsess and are driven to sins such as wasting time or worse due to the issue of Zionism. So do you want to be punished in the afterlife and possibly this life by doing something sinful to combat Zionism stupidly in a unislamic way that backfires and actually helps Zionism which you are ignorantly trying to defeat? Then when later generations do the right but difficult genuine Salafi religious revival that leads to the extinction of Zionism, possibly before prophet Jesus returns, as Allah decrees, you will not even be able to enjoy the news of the victory because of your regret at postponing it via your idiotic Anti-Zionism campaign that delayed true progress. For which you are also in pain as divinely ordered due to the sins earned by "combatting Zionism for the right reasons". If you are doing something for the right reasons then you can only do so if you do the right thing. It is possible to also do the right thing without having the right reasons too. But if you are doing the right thing, even if the results are slow to come or never come, if you truly do the right thing then that is the best thing for you. Sadly many believe they got the right intentions and are doing the right things too, but cannot prove this in the slightest and will be exposed to all by Allah to be wrong one way or another and treated as the wrongdoers they are. If individuals and groups started with the correct prophetic faith and stuck to it firmly the right methods to problem solve would be utilized by them. When they don't believe or practice Islamic Salafiyyah correctly then mistakes happen. Such as sinful hunger strikers starving to death or others burning themselves alive to "raise awareness". All such traps of Shaitan destroy and defeat people who think they are fighting evil not knowing Shaitan defeated them due to their extremist obsession and "solution" to just 1 of the devil's many plots.

So what am I doing about Zionism? That's not your concern. Our concern is what are we doing every second to worship Allah better? And if you got any concern other than pleasing Allah via your lifetime of worship then your soul has a much bigger problem than Zionism. For example, did Allah tell you to learn the latest news around the world once a day? No? What about once a week? If it's not a religious obligation why does it become such a constant habit when really important religious obligations are neglected? What do you do upon learning the recent news? Do your reactions impact events at all? If you are powerless to do something about the news you learn then why do you spend so much time and energy learning it? If X country and Y country are at war and you have no way to impact it and aren't even part of either side, what benefit did that information bring you? If you aren't a military soldier on X battlefield then what benefit do you get by learning about it? Some scholars of the Salaf would fear even hearing news of relevant battles during civil wars because they felt by inclining towards one side over the other they would be sinfully held as a partner in the bloodshed despite trying to maintain neutrality. So how about then when one enemy of Allah is fighting Zionism and the heart is torn between the parties automatically preferring one ally of

Shaitan over the other as in the case of the Shiite-Zionist "war" of recent times. So what benefit does learning the news bring anybody? Is learning news updates going to make you donate more, and pray more, and supplicate more than you would have otherwise? How is that? If you were such a strong enemy of devils why would learning about their latest crimes motivate you any extra to do good that you would've done anyways? Do you only supplicate for the Mujahideen, Scholars, Leaders, Raqis, Daees, during active combat? And if you don't hear any news then you give up doing good deeds fighting against evil? Do you only do good when the news motivates you and not when Allah commands it?

For a more pertinent example, people in far off lands hear of the blasphemously named Abraham Accords then they comment sinfully to vent emotional opinions on matters they cannot control and are not responsible for doing or improving. Yet when the same people are face to face with something they can control or influence like a local interfaith dawah event, those same loud mouth denouncers of Muslim rulers trying their best in a bad situation constantly made worse by millions of idiots globally, go with the flow when they are on or near the boat locally despite having nowhere near as much of a compelling reason locally to pay lip service to such a distortion of Abraham's pure Islamic faith. Those Muslim rulers see the Zionist Nuclear war machine pointed at them during diplomatic negotiating tables. But what mosque or dawah organization elsewhere has Jews and Christians coming to it with guns shooting and saying to hold an interfaith event, or else? Whereas such kufr is allowed to be stated with genuine violent compulsion but sinful gossip/protests/songs/pictures/rallies etc. are not lawful for most Anti-Zionist instances when these sins are done.

Muslim Scholars explained there are 4 conditions for compulsion to be genuine to warrant making a statement of kufr. Also know that this is just for statements of disbelief, actions of disbelief are not allowed except in extremely rare circumstances such as a Muslim spy infiltrating the ranks of an enemy army as a strategy of military warfare, not theological.

1. The compeller is actually able to perform that which he is threatening to do and the compelled one, who is commanded is unable to repel that even by fleeing.

2. That your assumption is certain that if you refuse then the compeller will fulfill the threat.

3. The threat is immediate and will be fulfilled on the spot.

4. Nothing indicates the excessiveness of the one compelled in giving into demands. Meaning only the minimum to remove the trial/danger/threat may be done. For example if someone is torturing you to say kufr/shirk then you can only say the absolute minimum that is

needed to stop the torture, not a single unislamic syllable more.

Quran 34:25

قُل لَّا تُسْـَٔلُونَ عَمَّآ أَجْرَمْنَا وَلَا نُسْـَٔلُ عَمَّا تَعْمَلُونَ (٢٥)

Say, "You will not be asked about what we committed, and we will not be asked about what you do." (25)

The reality of the trial of compromises made with Zionists is that everyone is responsible for themselves. If you are innocent of such unwanted positions then praise Allah for such protection. Yet when people criticize the errors of others and then go commit their own errors this causes problems to worsen. So if you are risky enough to bother spending any time learning global news on a frequent basis, despite not being qualified to do the right things to improve the headlines, then try to limit the debt of the addicting experience. Because you should fear losing your lifespan learning about news which doesn't concern you. Don't harm your soul playing such a futile game.

On the authority of Abu Hurairah who said the Messenger of Allah said,

"Part of the perfection of one's Islam is his leaving that which does not concern him."

Source: #12 of Nawwawi's 40 Hadith

Grade: Hasan

Whereas it is easily calculated that had ordinary Muslims outside of the Zionist violence zones spent 10 years ignoring such news and instead focused and strove hard in improving their Islam, then after those 10 years those Muslims would be much more able to actually do something about Zionism than if they spent 50 years learning the news of the Zionist expansion and constantly reacting to it. Do you think when soldiers train for the military to join a warzone battlefield that they spend time learning about the recent war news? No. They constantly prepare as much as they can for a war they plan to be in which they currently ignore, so that they can win the war later on the real violent battlefield. Thus those anti-Zionists who track the news of "their enemy" for motivation and strategy have already lost due to their strategy and weak motivation to actually fulfill their true purpose of existence. Your purpose of existence may clash with Zionism and other things overtime but such clashes can frighteningly corrupt you distracting you from you and your true life purpose. Of which a human like me where I am on earth and a human like you where you are both have identical purposes to worship Allah until death. Many of Allah's expectations are identically the same too. Yet nobody would expect us to both have the same actions even if it were possible for us to live nearly identical lives. Why? Because of the variables beyond our control, destined by Allah, greatly customizes our unique role despite having the same purpose and same prophetic legislation to follow. So it is entirely realistic that you may have a bigger problem in your journey to paradise to overcome than Zionism, which is specially unique to you. Therefore if you do your role as best as truly possible excelling with precise dedicated spiritual focus then you will see that for billions of creatures many popular world problems they are concerned with, are not valued correctly. This mistaken importance given to some problems over others causes a lot more problems making the world even more confusingly problematic. So pick your true unique problems and fix them to fix the world you live in.

For instance many "loyal devoted" Muslim friends of Allah can tell you a long list of names of the enemies of Allah. But how many names of Allah do they know? Likewise they can name many kafir villains but how many heroes like the Sahabah? They can quote the evil, hypocritical speeches and sayings of the devil's soldiers, but how many verses of Allah's book have they memorized and lived in obedience to?

We could go onwards if Allah wills but it seems the time used to write more beneficial words on this topic would not provide as much value as the time would if I spent it doing something else in obedience to Allah. For the major points of value seem to have been conveyed and additional expansion on the topic would be of diminishing value, especially on Judgement Day when my words and lifetime are weighed as to their worth in Allah's estimation.

As good a book as this may be I must focus on a more important book now; my personal lifetime Book of Deeds which the angels write exactly as I live it. Nobody in the grave will ever wish they could return to their life so they could've spent more time leaning global news. Rather all dead people wish they spent less time learning current news in their lifetime than they did and regret the precious time of life misspent. The

Sahaba who changed the world had this attitude of maximizing time value used during life to become better worshippers of Allah. They changed the world so much they became the news discussed by the world because of this super focus on sincere time spent doing good as prophetically instructed. So to minimize regret on the day of death and the Day of Judgement the sincere will gain the prophetic knowledge and live accordingly as if every second was an emergency gift from Allah. Truly this gift of life is lost with the passage of each second which will be either counted in your favor with a vast potential value range or it will count against you with a vast potential debt range on how much each wasted second will harm you. Rather than be concerned about the end of Zionism, concern yourself with your own life to become blessed instead of cursed.

NO PAGE IN YOUR BOOK OF DEEDS ON THE DAY OF TERROR SHOULD BE BLANK OR WASTED WITH SINS EVEN IF IT IS ERASED BY ALLAH DUE TO REPENTANCE.